Over 100 delicious recipes:

Tapas

Over 100 delicious recipes:
Tapas

Anja Werth

with recipes by
Food Look Studios

Photography by Brigitte Sporrer
and Alena Hrbkova

Notes

Eggs: Unless otherwise specified, use medium-sized eggs.

Milk: Unless otherwise specified, use whole milk (containing 3.5% milkfat).

Poultry: Poultry should always be well-cooked. To test whether it is cooked, insert a sharp knife in the thickest part of the thigh where it joins the body. If the juices run red or pink, allow a little more cooking time. If the juices runs clear, the poultry is done.

Nuts: A few recipes in this book contain nuts or nut oil as ingredients. If you are allergic to nuts or have a tendency to be, you should refrain from consuming these dishes.

Herbs: Unless otherwise indicated, always use fresh herbs. If they are not available they may be replaced by dried herbs but use smaller quantities.

Olive oil: The taste of olive oil differs vastly. We recommend two kinds of oils. Extra Virgin Olive Oil is best for preparing salads, crudités, sautéed vegetables or pasta dishes. It can be heated up to 180°C (350°F). Virgin Olive Oil is recommended for roasting and grilling (broiling). It may be heated up to 210°C (425°F). Olive oil should be stored at room temperature in a dark place.

Alcohol: Some recipes in this book contain alcohol. People suffering from alcohol-related problems, and children, should refrain from consuming these dishes.

Oven temperatures: The temperatures and cooking times refer to gas or electric ovens. If you have a fan oven, adjust the temperature according to the manufacturer's instructions.

Contents

INTRODUCTION

Good wining and dining are an integral part of the Spanish lifestyle. Their love of food has created a unique gastronomy, now recognised and enjoyed worldwide. *Tapas variadas* are the magic words of Spanish cuisine. They refer to all the tasty little hors d'oeuvres and appetizers that are enjoyed with wine or sherry in bars all over Spain at lunchtime and before dinner.

Years ago, *tapas* consisted only of some olives with a slice of sausage, ham or bread, but today there is usually a selection of a dozen or more *tapas* from which to choose.

Spicy tuna spreads, light scampi omelettes, delicious chicken breasts in sherry, sweet black pudding, fried cauliflower, grilled artichokes, chickpeas in vinaigrette, Moorish skewered meat ... these are just a few of the delicious tapa recipes to be found in the pages of this beautiful book.

It is only in Spain that the custom of serving irresistible appetizers with drinks has developed into a fine art and an important feature of everyday life. Wherever you go, in big cities or ancient villages, you will be offered *tapas* with your drink.

About tapas

Even *tapas* have their history and legends. Some people believe that they first appeared 700 years ago in the reign of Alfonso the Wise. He was so concerned about the drunkenness of his soldiers that he put lids (*tapas* in Spanish) with some titbits on top. The soldiers had to eat these before being allowed to drink.

Others believe that they are called *tapas* because they close the stomach and prevent blood alcohol levels rising. The fact that the Spanish, despite their regular indulgence in a quick aperitif, seldom appear to get drunk, tends to support this theory.

It is undisputed that *tapas*, which are part of everyday life in Spain, were first prepared in Andalucia. However, the tasty morsels were so popular that it was only a matter of time before they spread beyond Andalucia to the rest of Spain.

Andalusian delicacies

By the end of the nineteenth century, typical Andalucian wine bars, managed by gypsy families or mule drivers, were opened in Madrid. In the 1920s, there was a rapid growth of bars and wine taverns in Madrid, and numerous Flamenco stages opened. Andalucian culture – and, along with it, the *tapas* – made their entry.

This culinary custom has even created its own verb, reflecting its popularity. *Tapear* ('to fill up') refers to the popular Andalucian strolls whose sole destination is the best tapas bars, where you can enjoy some wine, a sherry or a beer while tasting these warm or cold gastronomic delicacies. An Eldorado for gourmets and food lovers, in these bars tapas are offered not only throughout the day but almost all night long as well.

Tapas and sherry make a match

Tapas are not *antipasti* in the real sense of the word. The small appetizers are closely linked to Spanish sherry. This drink was named by the English, who were incapable of pronouncing the word *Jerez* correctly (as in the Andalucian town of Jerez de la Frontera from which sherry derives its name). In Spain, sherry is still an everyday drink.

We know that the piece of bread, slice of ham or *cana de lomo* were placed over the sherry glass not just as protection against troublesome flies but also to retain the wonderful aroma in the glass. This, combined with the tendency of the Spanish to stand at a bar chatting with their friends, aquaintainces, family or the bartender over a snack or an aperitif, makes it easy for us to understand how pleasant and simple it is to lose track of time. In short, *tapas* complement the Spanish character and way of life. For the Spanish, they are much more than just a quick snack to eat – indeed, they are a way of communicating, almost a ritual.

Due to their integral role in everyday life, it is not altogether surprising that *tapas* also entered the realm of Spanish film-making. In every one of his

film productions, Pedro Almodóvar, the bad guy of Spanish film, insists on including scenes where *tapas* – the 'darling' of the Spanish – are being prepared.

A difficult choice

Today, *tapas* or *pinchos* (*pinchar* means 'to pinch'), as they are called in Northern Spain, are offered in many restaurants, tascas, bars and bodegas. When you order tapas in a bar they usually cut some bread first and serve it with your aperitif. Sometimes you may be offered bread with olive oil, or tomato and salt. A cut clove of raw garlic may be rubbed over the bread. Usually these simple *tapas* are 'on the house' – included in the price of your drink.

However, Jabugo, the most famous and delicious Spanish ham, makes a much more sophisticated appetizer. In good bars and restaurants, it is kept in a special rack and served skilfully cut with a sharp knife into very long, thin slices. This ham, with its distinctive flavour, makes a popular although expensive tapas dish.

The more extravagant *tapas* are displayed in bowls and dishes behind glass at the counter. Often there are a few dozen different warm or cold *tapas*, which are freshly prepared every day. They are usually served in *cazuelitas*, traditional brown earthenware dishes, or on small china plates. You can eat them either with a small fork or by skilfully using a tooth pick.

By the way, *tapas* are not to be confused with *bocadillos*. Compared to a *tapas*, a *bocadillo* is far more solid. In order to make a *bocadillo* a long loaf of white bread is sliced into 20 cm (8 inch) lengths and then cut in half. Usually, a little olive oil is drizzled over the cut surfaces, then the bread is toasted and finally spread with a layer of chopped or puréed tomatoes. Alternatively, it may be filled with an omelette or even some roast meat or fish.

A culinary experience: the regional specialties

Tapas vary greatly from region to region in Spain. Indeed, there are more than a dozen distinctive regional cuisines, each with their own *tapa* dishes, and these, in turn, are strongly influenced by the availability of local fresh ingredients. For instance, in Galicia, in northwest Spain, they have delicious veal dishes which are barely known in Andalucia in southern Spain. Asturias is famous for its cider (*sidra*), for its *fabada*, the legendary bean soup, and its *queso cabralés*, a savoury blue cheese. The Basque country is regarded as the gastronomic highlight of Spain. Fish specialities, such as *changurro* (stuffed crab), fish soups and *anguilas a la bilbaina* (baby eels in garlic), characterize the cuisine of the North. In the South, especially in Andalucia, it is the large prawns (shrimp) and *chanquetes* (tiny fried fish) that make your heart beat faster.

With the longest coast line of any European country, Spain offers a wide variety of fish and seafood. Combined with regional foods, such as round-grain rice from Valencia, delightful treats like *paella*, a Levanten speciality, are created.

Tortilla de patatas, Spain's popular potato omelette, is another speciality. This is thanks to the South American conquistadors, who brought back potatoes from Mexico to their homeland. Depending on the region and local preferences, it may be served either as a plain, rustic omelette or as a more sophisticated dish with green asparagus, tender ham or shrimps.

Soups and stews play an important role in Spanish cuisine, and, again, each region has its own special dishes. Inland, you can find sumptuous *cocidos* made with meat, ham and sausages, whereas the coastal regions offer wonderful shellfish and seafood stews. The most well-known version is the Catalonian *zarzuela*, named after the Spanish operetta. In the hot climate of Andalucia, a cool *gazpacho*, a tomato soup of infinite variety, can be delightfully refreshing on a hot summer's day.

In Spanish cuisine, poultry ranks second in popularity after fish. Presumably this dates back to the times when Spain was ruled by the Moors and eating pork was prohibited due to religious reasons.

On the Islands

The *tapas* ritual has spread from the Spanish mainland to the Canary Islands. In almost every bar

outside the main tourist areas you will find a variety of *tapas* served on very small plates, which is an excellent way of trying out different dishes. You can experiment with such appetizers as pork fried in *gofio* (flour made from ground roasted cereal grains), beef with potatoes, tun salad, chicken or vegetables char-grilled on a hot rack (*a la plancha*) and gambas (shrimp) with garlic, or with delectable 'nibbles' such as fried pork lard (*chicharrones*), almonds, fresh figs and dried fruits.

In Mallorca, too, these delicious hors d'oeuvres are part of everyday life. In good restaurants, the waiter usually asks: '*Algo para picar*?' meaning 'Would you like something to pick?' (referring to tapas). Even if soup or another first course is ordered instead, every guest is given some bread and olives, wild fennel and small, hot pickled chillies to complement his aperitif.

It is the availability of fresh high-quality ingredients and regional characteristics that influence the preparation and variety of tapas or pinchos. A few of these small delicacies are found everywhere – in Madrid as well as Seville – while others are offered only in certain cities or regions. Therefore, a gastronomic *tapas* round trip is a worthwhile experience for the seasoned gourmet.

A fixed menu

Nowadays, *tapas* have a permanent place on the daily menu, which is taken very seriously by the Spanish. A small breakfast, usually an espresso (*café solo*) or a coffee with milk (*café con leche*) with a piece of toast or a pastry, is consumed at home or in one of the many bars. The actual breakfast, the *almuerzo*, follows later on in the morning between 10 and 11 o'clock. Usually you have a coffee, which occasionally may be replaced by a glass of wine or sherry, together with some bread with olive oil and tomatoes, or, depending on the region, with butter and *jamón* (Spanish ham) and some olives.

Around 1 o'clock in the afternoon, the Spanish get ready for lunch. The first *tapas* together with a *fino*, a dry sherry, are ordered and consumed with small forks or tooth picks. Usually this scenario takes place

in a *tapas* bar just around the corner from their workplace, which can be found in every large town and small village. It is only in Spain that you get ready for lunch in this way. 'Lunch *tapas*' whet your appetite for the *comida*, the luncheon, which is served between 2 and 3 o'clock in the afternoon and consists of three courses – hors d'oeuvres, main course and dessert. If you are still hungry after that, you allow yourself a *merienda*, a short coffee break, with a pastry or sandwiches at around 6 pm .

Almost Cult: tapas bars

It is in the evenings – between 8 and 9 pm – that the *tapas* sampling of the morning is continued in one of the many tapas bars with friends after a hard day's work. To round off your glass of sherry, you can nibble at salted almonds, olives, Serrano ham, red pepper sausage (*chorizo*) and cheese. Or you can even try a few small cold and warm snacks, such as marinated vegetables and seafood, kidneys in sherry sauce, fried anchovies, crispy potato balls, finely marinated mushrooms, potato omelette (*tortilla española*), potatoes in garlic sauce (*patatas ali-oli*) and grilled shrimps (*gambas a la plancha*) to name but a few! These innumerable appetizers often replace the *entremeses*, the first course, which is of little importance in Spain.

Invariably, such an evening ends in a *tapeo*, a tapas tour from bar to bar. *Tapas* bars are the centre of social life in Spain but they have little in common with a British pub or an American bar except for the fact that people go there to drink. A Spanish bar is much more than a drinking place. Each *tapas* bar is keen to promote its own unique image and offers one or more tapas specialities. On market days, in particular, large quantities of these appetizers are displayed in glass counters.

Not suprisingly, after one of these *tapas* trips, some people abstain from dinner, which would normally follow at around 10 pm, and order – if they are still hungry – *raciones*, larger servings of the same *tapas* dishes which are usually served as appetizers. If you feel the urge for a late-night snack around midnight, you can visit a *bodega* or *tasca*.

The day never seems to end in Spain and there is always something *para picar* ('to pick'), as the Spanish say, for they never have a drink without a roast almond or a piece of cheese to accompany it. And, most important of all, they take all the time they need for this culinary ritual.

In the capital, this lifestyle is especially evident. Some visitors to Madrid may wonder how so many bars and restaurants which are so close to one another can possibly survive. Madrid, of course, offers the entire range of Spanish and international cuisine, yet *tapas* bars are the most important. There are many bars offering a range of up to 50 different *tapas*. One of the well-known specialities is the *chateo*, which is served traditionally with wine. *Chato* means 'snub nosed', and a 'chato' is a tour through the old taverns of Madrid, where you can drink wine out of snub-nosed glasses and enjoy all sorts of *tapas*.

Tapas – a trendy treat here as well

The Spanish *tapas* culture has attracted a growing and appreciative band of followers outside Spain. An increasing number of people in Britain, Europe ing these small appetizers, reminding them of their recent holidays. Today there are *tapas* bars in many big cities, their popularity proven by the numbers of eager gourmets clamouring at the bar. A good selection of *tapas* amply replaces a complete meal and nobody minds that these little Spanish teasers usually cost more than just a few pounds or dollars.

Making tapas is simple

Tapas are not only ideal party snacks, but as mixed *antipasti* they can also be served as a first course, as a light meal or a hearty midnight snack. They are easily prepared and suitable for all tastes. When using only really fresh ingredients, these home-made appetizers are a culinary feast. Even here you can find authentic ingredients such as Serrano ham, Manchego cheese and chorizo. Spanish delicatessens and even some large supermarkets offer a wide selection of speciality foods.

You will find the relevant recipes on the following pages. Apart from easy-to-prepare basic *tapas* dishes, there are recipes featuring fish, shellfish, meat and vegetables. With the help of this book, you can work miracles and serve endless *tapas* according to your guests' appetites and personal tastes. *Buen provecho* – enjoy your meal!

Basic Tapas

Newcomers to *tapas* cuisine are well advised to start with just a few basic tapas. In this chapter you will find everything you need for an interesting *tapas* platter. From simple to lavish *tapas*, using meat, fish, vegetables or cheese, various delicacies, such as eggs with chillies (see page 40), fried cheese cubes (see page 29) or spicy pickled olives (see page 27), are easily and quickly prepared and are sure to please your guests.

Pan con aceite y tomate
Bread with Oil and Tomato

This *tapas* dish should be included in every buffet. It is best with a selection of hams and sausages, cut into slices or small pieces. It is perfectly accompanied by olives, some white or granary bread and a glass of sherry.

White or wholemeal (wholewheat) bread

1 garlic clove

Olive oil

2 tomatoes

Salt

❶ Cut the bread into slices, at least 1 cm (1/2 inch) thick. Use fresh bread or toast it, if preferred.

❷ Peel the garlic clove and cut in half. Rub over the bread and drizzle with some olive oil.

❸ Wash the tomatoes, remove the stems, cut in half and rub onto the bread. Sprinkle lightly with salt and serve.

Serves 4, about 220 kcal per serving

Pan con tomate y jamón
Tomato Bread with Ham

The original version of this bread – *Pa amb Oli*, or bread with oil – is a favourite in Mallorca. It is also served with richer toppings, such as fish, sausage or ham. However, the basic dish always consists of a slice of bread, spread with mashed tomatoes and then drizzled with olive oil.

4 ripe plum tomatoes

2 garlic cloves

4 slices of crusty wholemeal (wholewheat) bread

Salt and freshly ground black pepper

4 tablespoons olive oil

8 thin slices Serrano ham

8 black olives, pickled in salt and drained

❶ Put the tomatoes in a bowl, pour boiling water over them and leave for 1 minute. Remove the tomatoes, skin, remove the stems, cut in half, deseed and pour away the juice. Mash the tomatoes with a fork. The purée should not be too juicy.

❷ Peel the garlic cloves and cut in half. Toast the bread slices and rub with the garlic halves while still warm. Spread the tomato mash over the bread and season with salt and pepper. Drizzle 1 tablespoon of olive oil over each slice of bread.

❸ Place 2 slices of Serrano ham on each piece of bread and garnish with some black olives.

Serves 4, about 350 kcal per serving

Gambas al ajillo
Gambas with Garlic

This recipe originally comes from Asturias, more precisely from Cantabria. It is well-known throughout Spain and served in many *tapas* bars. You can vary it by adding chopped parsley, using more garlic or, if you prefer, less chilli.

500 g/ 1 lb fresh small prawns (shrimp)

1 fresh red chilli

5 garlic cloves

Olive oil

1 bay leaf (optional)

Sea salt

Freshly ground black pepper

2 tablespoons finely chopped parsley

❶ Shell the prawns (shrimp), and remove the black vein running along the back of each one.

❷ Slice the red chilli lengthways, deseed and cut into thin half-rings. Peel the garlic clove and slice thinly.

❸ Cover the bottom of a pan with 1 cm ($\frac{1}{2}$ inch) olive oil and place over a low heat – the oil should not smoke but it should be as hot as possible.

❹ Add the garlic, chilli, prawns (shrimp) and bay leaf (if using) to the hot oil and fry at a high temperature for 2 minutes, stirring constantly with a wooden spoon. Season to taste with salt and pepper.

❺ Sprinkle with parsley just before serving.

Serves 4, about 410 kcal per serving

Gambas rebozadas
Fried Gambas

This classic tapa dish originates from the Levante, but has spread throughout the rest of Spain and can now be found everywhere. The recipe is simple – only the batter dough differs. There are a dozen 'top secret recipes' for this speciality, but they should all be crisp on the outside and juicy inside.

12 large prawns (jumbo shrimps)

100 g/3¹/₂ oz (1 cup) plain (all-purpose) flour

Salt

Freshly ground white pepper

100 ml 3¹/₂ fl oz (¹/₂ cup) beer

Olive oil

1 egg white

A few lemon wedges

❶ Dip the prawns (shrimp) into boiling water for a few seconds. Peel them down to the tail, and remove the heads and black vein along the spine with a sharp knife. Pat dry with kitchen paper (paper towels).

❷ Mix the flour with the salt and pepper in a bowl.

❸ Gradually stir the beer, warmed with 100 ml/3¹/₂ fl oz (¹/₂ cup) water and 2 tablespoons oil into the seasoned flour. Beat with a wire whisk until smooth and creamy.

❹ In a clean, dry bowl, beat the egg white until stiff and fold gently into the batter. Heat the olive oil (about two fingers high) in a heavy pan.

❺ Dip the prepared prawns (shrimp) into the batter, holding them by their tails. Fry immediately in the hot oil until golden brown, then remove and drain on kitchen paper (paper towels).

❻ Serve hot, garnished with lemon wedges, with a glass of dry sherry.

Serves 4, about 190 kcal per serving

Boquerones victorianos
Fried Sardines

When marinating sardines for a *tapas* buffet, set one or two dozen aside and fry them. Even marinated sardines can be deep-fried. Serve with mayonnaise or aioli.

❶ Wash the sardines, pat dry with kitchen paper (paper towels) and dust lightly with flour.

❷ Heat the olive oil (two fingers high) in a heavy pan and fry the sardines and bay leaf. Drain on kitchen paper (paper towels) and add a pinch of salt.

❸ Serve immediately with lemon quarters.

Serves 4, about 230 kcal per serving

50 g/2 oz sardines

Flour

Olive oil

1 bay leaf

A pinch of salt

2 organic lemons, cut into quarters

Aceitunas en adobo
Spiced and Pickled Olives

Pickled olives are an ideal addition to *pan con aceite y tomate* and to ham and sausages, including the *Embutidos*, such as *Butifarrón* (black pudding) or *Sobresada* (spicy pork sausage) which is very popular in Catalonia and the Balearics. They also go well with chorizo, the spicy Spanish sausage, which is always delicious whether it is served cold, grilled or dropped into a *fabada* (white bean stew).

❶ Crush the olives with the broad blade of a large kitchen knife until they are flat. Place in a cooking jar or a bowl. Peel the garlic cloves and chop finely.

❷ Sprinkle the olives with garlic, fennel seeds, marjoram and rosemary.

❸ Add the chilli powder, salt and freshly ground pepper, then cover with olive oil. Stir or shake and leave to marinate for several days.

Serves 4, about 170 kcal per serving

500 g/1 lb medium-sized olives, pickled in vinegar

5 garlic cloves

1 sprig of marjoram

1 sprig of rosemary

1 teaspoon fennel seeds

1 teaspoon hot chilli powder

Salt and freshly ground black pepper

Olive oil

Bollos de Cuajad
Cream Cheese Balls

This *tapas* dish, which does not contain salt, originated in Asturias. A similar recipe, not fried and coated with honey, is known in Catalonia. Its basic ingredient is always cream cheese or yogurt, or a mixture of both. Either sheep's or cow's milk may be used.

1 Mix the cream cheese, eggs, lemon rind, nutmeg and sifted flour.

2 Heat the olive oil in a heavy pan to 180°C (350°F).

3 Form the cream cheese mixture into 3–4 cm (1–1½ inch) diameter balls and fry them in the hot oil until crisp. Remove with a slotted spoon, drain on kitchen paper (paper towels) and serve.

Serves 4, about 500 kcal per serving

1 kg/2 lb cream cheese

8 eggs

Grated rind of 1 lemon, organically grown

Pinch of grated nutmeg

50 g/2 oz (½ cup) flour, sifted

Olive oil

Queso frito
Fried Cheese Cubes

Manchego, a sheep's milk cheese from the La Mancha region with a strong flavour, is used for this tapas dish. However, other hard or semi-hard cheeses may be used instead. The hot cheese cubes are served as appetizers together with green grapes and an aperitif.

1 Remove the rind from the cheese and then dice the cheese into 2 cm (1 inch) cubes.

2 Beat the eggs with the cream in a bowl. Mix the cornmeal with the ground almonds in another bowl. Sift the flour into a shallow dish.

3 Roll the cheese cubes first in the flour, then coat with the beaten egg and, finally, roll in the cornmeal and almond mixture.

4 Heat the olive oil in a large pan and fry the cheese cubes in batches until golden brown. Drain on kitchen paper (paper towels) and serve hot.

Serves 4, about 350 kcal per serving

400 g/14 oz Spanish Manchego cheese, or other medium-hard to hard cheese

2 eggs

1 teaspoon double (heavy) cream

50 g/2 oz (⅓ cup) cornmeal

50 g/2 oz (½ cup) ground almonds

Flour

250 ml/8 fl oz (1 cup) olive oil

Prebes coents
Marinated Peppers

Marinated vegetables are a classic in Mediterranean cuisine. The olive oil and vinegar should be of excellent quality to enhance the delicious flavour of this *antipasto* dish.

250 g/8 oz red (bell) peppers

250 g/8 oz yellow (bell) peppers

3 tablespoons wine vinegar

Salt and freshly ground black pepper

3 garlic cloves

6 tablespoons olive oil

½ bunch of fresh basil

½ bunch of fresh oregano

❶ Wash the peppers and roast in a preheated oven at 230°C (450°F), Gas Mark 8 until charred and blistered.

❷ Remove the peppers and wrap in a damp cloth. Leave to cool and then skin. Cut the peppers in half, remove the seeds and slice roughly.

❸ Mix the wine vinegar with the salt and pepper. Peel the garlic clove, slice thinly and add to the vinegar. Whisk in the olive oil.

❹ Place the peppers in a bowl and pour the marinade over them. Wash the basil and oregano and chop the leaves finely. Add to the peppers and leave to marinate in a cool place for 5 hours.

Serves 4–6, about 150–200 kcal per serving

Pimientos y calabacines con ajilimoje

Peppers and Courgettes (Zucchini) with Aioli

Peppers are a basic element in Spanish cuisine. This recipe is easily prepared and tastes delicious all the year round. Spicy aioli is perfect with marinated vegetables. The Spanish love to eat this with grilled (broiled) fish or meat.

❶ Wash the peppers and courgettes (zucchini), remove the stems, quarter them lengthwise and deseed. Pour 100 ml/3½ fl oz (1½ cup) olive oil into a baking dish and spread the vegetables over it.

❷ Peel the garlic clove and chop finely. Sprinkle the garlic and pepper over the vegetables and drizzle with lemon juice.

❸ Cook in a preheated oven at 220°C (425°F), Gas Mark 7 for about 20 minutes. Check after 15 minutes to see if the vegetables are tender.

❹ Remove the peppers and courgettes (zucchini) from the oven and place in a shallow bowl. While hot, sprinkle with sherry vinegar. Cover and leave to marinate in the refrigerator for at least 3 hours.

❺ Mix together the mayonnaise and crème fraîche. Peel the garlic cloves, crush and stir into the mayonnaise cream with the lemon juice. It is best to prepare the aioli just before serving. Serve with some crusty bread and the marinated vegetables.

Serves 4, about 500 kcal per serving

2 large red (bell) peppers
2 large yellow (bell) peppers
2 courgettes (zucchini)
100 ml/3½ fl oz (½ cup) olive oil
4 garlic cloves
3 teaspoons lemon juice
Freshly ground black pepper
3 tablespoons sherry vinegar

For the Aioli:
4 tablespoons mayonnaise
2 tablespoons crème fraîche
3 garlic cloves
1 tablespoon lemon juice

Migas
Toasted White Bread Cubes

Migas are very easily prepared and go well with an aperitif. They are essential for any *tapas* buffet.

5–6 slices stale white bread

Good pinch of chilli powder

4–5 tablespoons olive oil

100 g/3¹/₂ oz smoked bacon

2 garlic cloves

1 fresh chilli

❶ Remove the crusts from the bread, cut the bread into cubes and place them in a bowl.

❷ Spray the bread cubes with water on all sides until the bread is moist but not too damp.

❸ Stir the chilli powder into the bread cubes until lightly coated. Cover the bowl and set aside for 2 hours.

❹ Cut the bacon into cubes. Peel the garlic clove and chop finely.

❺ Heat the olive oil in a pan and slowly fry the bacon cubes. Add the garlic and chilli.

❻ Add the bread cubes to the pan and sauté until golden brown, stirring constantly.

Serves 4, about 440 kcal per serving

Boquerones en vinagre
Marinated Sardines

You can buy fresh sardines at most fishmongers and fresh fish counters in supermarkets. In Spanish markets, marinated sardines are often sold from small plastic barrels. Originally a Levanten speciality, they have now become a standard *tapas* dish everywhere in Spain. The recipe requires some patience and skill, but is well worth the effort.

1 Wash the sardines, slice through the belly with a sharp knife and open up. Press each sardine out flat with the wide blade of a large kitchen knife. Remove the bones and head. Rinse the sardines thoroughly under running cold water, pat dry and press flat again.

2 Place the sardines in 2–3 layers in a large, shallow bowl, belly-side up.

3 Mix the sherry vinegar with 100 ml/3½ fl oz (½ cup) water and pour over the sardines. Leave to marinate for about 2 hours until the flesh lightens. Rinse again under running cold water, then pat dry and dip each sardine into some more sherry vinegar and water (half and half) and pat dry with kitchen paper (paper towels).

4 Lay the sardines once again in the bowl. Peel the garlic cloves and chop finely.

5 Chop the parsley coarsely, mix with the sea salt, pepper and olive oil and pour over the sardines.

Serves 8, about 110 kcal per serving

500 g/1 lb fresh sardines
2 tablespoons sherry vinegar
6–7 garlic cloves
1 small bunch of flat-leaf parsley
Sea salt
Freshly ground black pepper
Olive oil

Almejas al jerez
Scallops in Sherry

❶ Wash the scallops thoroughly under running cold water. Pour some boiling water over the tomatoes in a bowl, then skin and remove the stems. Cut each tomato in half and scoop out the seeds. Press the tomato seeds and juices through a fine sieve into a small bowl and add the saffron threads. Set aside.

❷ Dice the tomato flesh. Peel the onion and chop finely.

❸ Cover the bottom of a deep saucepan with olive oil and place over a high heat. Peel the garlic cloves and fry the whole in the hot oil. Add the chopped onion, then the diced tomato and fry quickly until softened.

❹ Add the scallops and cook for 2–3 minutes, stirring constantly. Then add the tomato pulp and saffron threads.

❺ After 1 minute, pour the sherry over the scallop mixture and leave to cook over a low heat for about 5–7 minutes, according to the size of the scallops. Season to taste with salt and pepper, and sprinkle with parsley just before serving. This dish goes well with some dry white wine.

Serves 4, about 190 kcal per serving

500 g/1 lb scallops

1 large ripe tomato

2 saffron threads

1 large white onion

Olive oil

2–3 garlic cloves

2 teaspoons dry sherry

Sea salt

Freshly ground white pepper

2 tablespoons finely chopped parsley

Almendras Saladas
Salted Almonds

These almonds are perfect for entertaining at home or as a 'nibble' at parties. Their unique taste is superior to that of commercially produced counterparts. The quality of the almonds is, of course, very important. We suggest you use Spanish rather than Californian almonds. Although they are more difficult to peel and have an irregular shape, their taste is incomparable. This dish is considered one of the essential basic *tapas*, along with olives.

1 Place the almonds in a pan of boiling water for 10–15 seconds, then peel. Leave to dry on a kitchen cloth overnight.

2 Pour 2.5 cm (1 inch) olive oil into a heavy-based pan and heat until it is hot but not smoking. Fry the almonds until they turn a light golden brown. Remove from the oil with a slotted spoon as soon as they start to colour. They will turn even darker.

3 Leave to drain on kitchen paper (paper towels) and then pat dry. Sprinkle with coarse sea salt before serving.

Serves 4, about 175 kcal per serving

100 g/3^1/$_2$ oz (^{2}/$_3$ cup) almonds (Spanish, if possible)

Olive oil

Coarse sea salt

Almejas al ajillo
Scallops in Garlic Sauce

Scallops have particularly beautiful shells and are sometimes known as Coquilles St. Jacques. They are the symbol of the pilgrims visiting the grave of Jacobus, the apostle, in Santiago de Compostela. The meat of the scallop is extremely tender.

1 kg/2 lb scallops in shells

5 garlic cloves

1 spring onion (scallion), finely chopped

5 tablespoons olive oil

1 fresh red chilli

200 ml/7 fl oz (7/8 cup) white wine

2 tablespoons lemon juice

2 tablespoons finely chopped basil

❶ Wash and scrub the scallop shells thoroughly under running cold water. Never use scallops that are already open.

❷ Peel the garlic cloves and chop finely. Sauté in the olive oil with the spring onion (scallion). Add the chilli, then pour the white wine and 125 ml/4 fl oz (5/8 cup) water over it. Add the lemon juice and basil.

❸ Bring to the boil, then add the scallops, cover the pan and simmer over a low heat for 10 minutes. Stir once or twice to ensure that the scallops cook evenly.

❹ Discard any scallops that do not open while cooking – they are not edible. Serve the hot scallops in their sauce, together with some fresh white bread.

Serves 4, about 440 kcal per serving

Canadillas con vinagre
Marinated Sea Snails

Canadillas is the name of the large sea snails, armoured with bristles, that are very popular on the Spanish coast because of their exquisite taste. However, if you cannot get any sea snails, use fresh scallops instead.

❶ Cut the chilli in half, deseed and chop finely. Add with the peppercorns, coriander seeds and bay leaf to the sherry vinegar. Leave to marinate overnight in a cool place.

❷ Wash the sea snails thoroughly under running cold water. Cook in sufficient water for 20–30 minutes, according to size. Wash again.

❸ Pour the marinade over the sea snails while they are still warm and stir several times.

❹ Leave to cool and serve with dry sherry.

Serves 4, about 150 kcal per serving

1 large red chilli

12 white peppercorns

1 teaspoon coriander seeds

1 bay leaf

500 ml/17 fl oz (2¼ cups) sherry vinegar

24 large sea snails or scallops

Dátiles con bacon
Dates with Bacon

This exquisite date recipe comes from Andalusia. Make sure that the dried dates are not too old and are of excellent quality; otherwise they tend to become dry whilst you are preparing the dish.

❶ Cut the bacon rashers (slices) in half.

❷ Firmly wrap half a slice of bacon around each date and secure with a cocktail stick (toothpick).

❸ Heat the olive oil with the 2 peeled garlic cloves until it is hot but not smoking.

❹ Fry the bacon-wrapped dates until the bacon is crisp and golden brown, then season with salt and pepper.

Serves 4, about 360 kcal per serving

12 rashers (slices) smoked bacon

24 dried dates, stoned (pitted)

Olive oil

2 garlic cloves, peeled

Salt and freshly ground pepper

24 cocktail sticks (toothpicks)

Piparrada
Eggs and Peppers

Ripe (bell) peppers and tomatoes are required for this pepper omelette. Unripe vegetables might give the *piparrada* a slightly bitter flavour. This dish can be found in many tapas bars in the Basque country.

1 onion

2 garlic cloves

2 (bell) peppers (red or green)

3 tablespoons olive oil

8 tomatoes

80/3 oz g Serrano or raw ham (not too heavily salted), thinly sliced

3 eggs

Salt

Freshly ground white pepper

❶ Wash and deseed the peppers and cut into strips. Peel the onions and garlic cloves and chop finely.

❷ Heat the olive oil in a pan. Sauté the onions until softened, then add the garlic and peppers and cook gently for about 5 minutes.

❸ Pour some boiling water over the tomatoes, then skin, remove the stems and seeds and cut into dice. Add to the pan with the ham and sauté over a medium heat until the tomatoes are creamy. Season to taste with salt and pepper.

❹ Beat the eggs with a fork in a small bowl. Spread out the pepper, tomato and ham mixture evenly across the bottom of the pan and pour in the beaten eggs. Do not stir.

❺ Leave to cook gently over a low heat until the omelette has set underneath. Finish cooking under a preheated grill (broiler) to cook the top. Slide the omelette out onto a plate just before serving.

Serves 4, about 280 kcal per serving

Huevos a la Sóller
Eggs Sóller

Sóller is the name of a port in Mallorca which traditionally has strong links with France. It is probable that the mashed vegetables, on which the *Huevos a la Sóller* are served, originated in France.

1 Peel the carrots, clean the leeks and wash thoroughly. Cut into small pieces and cook together in a pan with the peas and a little water for about 20 minutes until tender.

2 Drain the cooked vegetables, saving the cooking water. Return to the pan, add the cream and a little of the cooking water and mash wiht a potato masher or fork until smooth. Season to taste with nutmeg, salt and pepper. Keep warm in a low oven.

3 Fry the Sobrasada in the olive oil in a large pan. Drain on kitchen paper (paper towels) and keep warm together with the mash.

4 Use the same pan to fry the eggs, constantly basting them with the hot oil.

5 Serve the mash with 2 slices of *Sobrasada* and 2 fried eggs per person.

Serves 4, about 630 kcal per serving

2 large carrots

4 small leeks

300 g/10 oz (2¹/₂ cups) frozen peas

100 ml/3¹/₂ fl oz (¹/₂ cup) double (heavy) cream

Ground nutmeg

Salt

Freshly ground white pepper

8 slices *Sobrasada* (spicy sausage)

Olive oil

8 large eggs

Queso Mahonés al perejil
Mahon Cheese with Parsley

This *tapas* recipe is a speciality from the island of Menorca which is famous for its cheese from Mahón. It is prepared with local hard or semi-hard cheeses in many other parts of Spain, too.

❶ Cut the cheese into 2.5 cm (1 inch) cubes and roll in the cornmeal. Wash the parsley and chop the leaves finely.

❷ Beat the eggs with 1 tablespoon milk and dip the cheese cubes into this mixture. Then coat once more with cornmeal.

❸ Heat the olive oil (two fingers high) in a pan and fry the coated cheese cubes until golden brown.

❹ Remove and dry on kitchen paper (paper towels) for a short time, then roll in the finely chopped parsley. Serve warm.

Serves 4, about 320 kcal per serving

200 g/7 oz Mahon cheese (or any other hard cheese)

100 g/3$^{1}/_{2}$ oz ($^{1}/_{2}$ cup) cornmeal

2 eggs

2 tablespoons milk

1 bunch of flat-leaf parsley

Olive oil

Salt

Pimientos al horno o a la brasa

Roasted Peppers

In Navarra and the Basque country in northern Spain, slices of pepper are fried and seasoned with chilli when no fully ripe red peppers are available. In this variation, the peppers are roasted and marinated in a garlic-flavoured sherry vinegar.

4 large red (bell) peppers

4 garlic cloves

Sherry vinegar

Salt

Freshly ground white and black pepper

Olive oil

❶ Preheat the oven to 230°C (450°F), Gas Mark 8. Wash the peppers, dry and roast in the oven for 15–20 minutes until they blister and the skin turns dark brown to black.

❷ Remove the peppers, skin, deseed and cut into thick strips (about the thickness of a finger).

❸ While the peppers are roasting, peel the garlic cloves, cut into thin strips and marinate in the sherry vinegar.

❹ Add the peppers while still slightly warm and turn in the marinade. Season with salt and pepper and drizzle with olive oil.

Serves 4, about 130 kcal per serving

Fish Tapas

If you prefer fish and seafood you will enjoy these recipes. From fish croquettes (see page 50), to scallops with parsley (see page 66) or squid with young beans (see page 65), there is a *tapas* dish for everybody. Whether it is for an elegant dinner, a party or a midnight snack, fish or seafood make delicious appetizers.

Albóndigas de bacalao
Cod Balls

The Arabic influence endows this recipe with an extraordinary flavour. It adds an element of surprise to any tapas buffet table. For a really authentic flavour, you should buy only large dried cod fillets.

For the balls:

300 g/10 oz dried cod fillets

1 bay leaf

500 ml/17 fl oz (2¼ cups) milk

250 ml/8 fl oz (1 cup) natural (plain) yogurt

½ bunch of flat-leaf parsley

A pinch of ground cinnamon

2 eggs

Freshly ground white pepper

50 g/2 oz (1 cup) fresh white breadcrumbs

Olive oil

For the sauce:

30 g/1 oz (¼ cup) almonds

30 g/1 oz (¼ cup) hazelnuts

2–3 tablespoons olive oil

3 slices white bread

4 garlic cloves

200 ml/7 fl oz (⅞ cup) fish stock (broth)

100 ml/3½ fl oz (½ cup) dry white wine

2 saffron threads

❶ Skin the cod fillets and remove any bones. Remove the fins and set aside. Cut the fillets into cubes and leave to soak in some water together with a bay leaf. Change the water several times during the day. Mix the fish cubes with 250 ml/8 fl oz (1 cup) of the milk and the yogurt and leave to soak overnight.

❷ The following day, rinse again under running water. Wash and finely chop the parsley leaves. Mix the cod with the parsley, cinnamon, eggs, white pepper, the remaining milk and breadcrumbs. Whizz in a blender until smooth.

❸ Form the mixture into small balls, about 2.5 cm (1 inch) thick. Heat some olive oil in a pan and fry the cod balls until golden brown. Place in an ovenproof dish or roasting pan.

❹ To make the sauce, fry the almonds and hazelnuts in the olive oil until golden brown. Remove and drain, and then fry the slices of bread. Peel the garlic cloves and crush finely.

❺ Mix together the nuts, garlic and white bread with the stock (broth), white wine and saffron threads and purée in the unwashed blender. Transfer to a pan and bring to the boil.

❻ Pour the sauce over the cod balls and bake in a preheated oven at 170°C (325°F), Gas Mark 3 for 15–20 minutes.

Serves 4, about 700 kcal per serving

Croquetas de bacalao
Cod Croquettes

In Spain, cod is used to make these delicious croquettes. However, you could substitute haddock, monkfish (anglerfish) or another white fish. The croquettes are seasoned with aromatic herbs and capers before frying in hot oil.

350 g/12 oz cod fillets

2 tablespoons lemon juice

3 teaspoons crème fraîche

2 garlic cloves

1 spring onion (scallion)

1 stale bread roll

2 eggs

Salt

2 teaspoons capers

1 tablespoon chopped parsley

1 tablespoon chopped dill

1 tablespoon chopped thyme

Freshly ground white pepper

Fresh breadcrumbs

Olive oil

1 lemon, organically grown

❶ Wash the fish fillets and pat dry with kitchen paper(paper towels). Cut into pieces, drizzle with lemon juice and then process with the crème fraîche in a blender or food processor.

❷ Peel the garlic cloves and chop them finely with the spring onion (scallion). Crumble the bread roll coarsely and add, together with the garlic mixture, to the fish. Beat the eggs, season with a little salt and carefully fold into the fish mixture with a fork.

❸ Chop the capers finely and add to the fish mixture with the herbs and pepper. With wet hands, form the mixture into croquettes, about 8 cm (3 inches) long and 4 cm (1¹/₂ inches) thick.

❹ Coat the croquettes in breadcrumbs. Heat sufficient olive oil in a heavy pan and fry the croquettes over a medium heat until golden brown. Cut the lemon into 8 wedges and serve with the hot croquettes.

Serves 4, about 280 kcal per serving

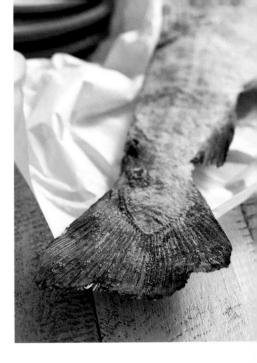

Fritos de pescado
Fried Fish Fritters

Crisp-fried cod and haddock fillets are the best fish to use for this dish, although monkfish (anglerfish) is also suitable. The fillets are cut into strips, coated with breadcrumbs and fried.

❶ Rinse the fish fillets, pat dry with kitchen paper (paper towels), slice in half lengthways and cut across into pieces (about the size of your thumb).

❷ Place the fish fillets on a plate, drizzle with lemon juice, season with a little salt and then set aside for 10 minutes.

❸ Beat the eggs. Prepare 3 shallow bowls for coating the fish: one with flour, one with beaten egg, and the third with breadcrumbs. Pat the fish dry with kitchen paper (paper towels, then coat lightly with flour. Dip the floured fish into the beaten egg and, finally, coat with breadcrumbs.

❹ Heat the oil in a deep pan or deep-fryer to about 180°C (350°F). Lower the fish, a few at a time, into the hot oil (it should not be too hot) and fry until crisp all over. Remove and drain quickly on kitchen paper (paper towels) while you fry the rest of the fish. Cut the lemons into 8 wedges.

❺ Serve the fried fish on a preheated plate, garnished with lemon wedges and sprigs of parsley.

Serves 4, about 290 kcal per serving.

300 g/10 oz cod or haddock
   fillets

3 tablespoons lemon juice

Salt

2 eggs

3 tablespoons flour

125 g/4 oz (³/₄ cup) dried
   breadcrumbs

250 ml/8 fl oz (1 cup) vegetable
   oil for frying

1 lemon, organically grown

Sprigs of parsley, to garnish

Sardinas con tomate
Sardines with Tomatoes

Garlic and orange rind are the ingredients that give this interesting sardine recipe from Andalucia its very own distinctive flavour.

1 Wash and scale the sardines under running cold water. Fillet by removing the head, tail and spine. Cut each fillet in half.

2 Peel the garlic cloves and crush with the grated orange and lemon rind. Heat the olive oil in a heavy-based pan over a medium heat and fry the sardines on both sides. Remove and keep warm in a low oven.

3 Add the garlic mixture to the pan and fry quickly. Add the sherry. Immerse the tomatoes briefly in boiling water, then skin and chop. Add to the pan and leave to simmer over a low heat for about 10 minutes.

4 Wash the basil, chop the leaves finely and add to the tomato mixture.

5 Pour the tomato sauce over the warm sardines. A chilled glass of sherry goes best with this typical Andalucian *tapas* dish.

Serves 4, about 270 kcal per serving

10 fresh sardines

2 garlic cloves

Grated rind of ½ orange,
   organically grown

A little grated lemon rind,
   organically grown

Olive oil

1½ tablespoons sherry

3 tomatoes

½ bunch of basil

Merluza a la sidra
Hake with Cider

This recipe hails from the Basque country where it is often prepared with monkfish (anglerfish) or cod. However, cod flakes easily and will not hold its shape. The fish may also be cubed and threaded onto skewers.

500 g/1 lb hake or monkfish (anglerfish)

Flour for coating

2 eggs

Olive oil

1 small onion

2 saffron threads

200 ml/7 fl oz ($7/8$ cup) dry cider

Salt

Freshly ground black pepper

❶ Rinse the fish and pat dry with kitchen paper (paper towels). Cut into serving portions, coat with flour and then dip into beaten egg.

❷ Heat sufficient olive oil in a heavy pan and fry the fish until crisp and golden. Remove with a slotted spoon and set aside.

❸ Heat 1 tablespoon olive oil in a pan. Peel and chop the onions, then sauté in the oil until softened.

❹ Add the saffron threads and cider. Bring to the boil, then add the fried fish pieces and reduce the heat.

❺ Simmer over a medium heat for 5 minutes. Season before serving.

Serves 4, about 320 kcal per serving

Empanadas de atún
Tuna Pies

Spanish bakeries – with their enticing aroma – sell not only sweet pastries but also little savoury pies, which are filled with fish, meat or vegetables, for when you are feeling peckish. These *empanadas* are easy to make at home.

For the dough:

350 g/12 oz (3¼ cups) plain (all-purpose) flour

1 teaspoon salt

175 g/6 oz (¾ cup) butter

1 egg

For the filling:

1 onion

1 garlic clove

2 tablespoons olive oil

1 small red (bell) pepper

1 small green (bell) pepper

1 tomato

250 g/8 oz can tuna in olive oil

Salt

Freshly ground black pepper

1 egg yolk

❶ Sift the flour and salt into a large bowl. Rub in the butter with your fingertips and then beat in the egg. Form the dough into a ball and chill for 30 minutes. Roll out the dough on a board dusted lightly with flour. Cut out circles, 10–15 cm (4–6 inches) in diameter with a cup or saucer.

❷ Peel the onion and garlic clove, chop finely and sauté in the oil until softened. Wash the peppers, deseed and dice. Wash the tomato, remove the stem, deseed and chop finely. Add the peppers and tomato to the onion mixture. Soften, then remove from the heat and cool for 5 minutes.

❸ Drain the tuna and cut into small pieces. Stir gently into the tomato mixture. Season to taste with salt and freshly ground pepper.

❹ Spread a tablespoon of the filling onto each circle of dough. Fold the dough over the top to form a semi-circle and press down firmly around the edges to seal each pie.

❺ Place the pies on a greased baking (cookie) sheet, brush with egg yolk and bake for 20–30 minutes in a preheated oven at 200°C (400°F), Gas Mark 6 until golden brown.

Serves 4, about 850 kcal per serving

Sardinas a la Santanderina
Coated Sardines Santander-Style

Spain has the longest coastline in Europe, and everybody knows the best ways to prepare and cook fish. Consequently, even a tapas recipe such as this can be a revelation. This recipe is a culinary celebration of the humble sardine.

❶ If not already filleted, cut the sardines into fillets. Clean under running cold water, rinse and pat dry with kitchen paper (paper towels).

❷ Wash the parsley and chop the leaves finely. Peel the garlic cloves and chop finely. Mix the parsley and garlic with the breadcrumbs. Coat the sardine fillets first in olive oil, then in breadcrumbs.

❸ Arrange the sardines side by side, not overlapping, on a lightly greased baking (cookie) sheet. Season lightly with salt.

❹ Bake in a preheated oven at 180°C (350°F), Gas Mark 4 for 10 minutes until golden brown. Turn the sardines over and cook the other side.

❺ Wash the lemons and cut one into 8 wedges. Squeeze the other lemon and sprinkle the juice over the sardines. Serve hot with lemon wedges.

Serves 4, about 350 kcal per serving

500 g/1 lb fresh sardine fillets (about 1 kg/2lb fresh whole sardines)

1 bunch of flat-leaf parsley

3 garlic cloves

100 g/3¹/₂ oz (1¹/₂ cups) fresh white breadcrumbs

Olive oil

Salt

2 lemons, organically grown

Chocos con habas
Squid with Broad (Fava) Beans

This unusual dish came originally from the Atlantic coast of Andalucia. The squid from this region are particularly tender and flavoursome. If fresh squid are not available, you can use frozen squid instead.

❶ Cut the squid, along with the tentacles, into serving portions.

❷ Heat the olive oil in a heavy pan and add 4 unpeeled garlic cloves. Peel and slice the remaining 2 cloves, then sauté in the hot oil with the pieces of squid for about 8 minutes.

❸ Add the shelled broad (fava) beans.

❹ Pour some fish stock (broth) over the squid and beans. Cover and leave to simmer for about 20 minutes, adding more liquid if necessary.

❺ Halfway through cooking, add the marjoram leaves, stripped from the stem. Season to taste with salt and pepper.

Serves 4, about 500 kcal per serving

500 g/1 lb small squid, cleaned

Olive oil

6 garlic cloves

300 g/10 oz broad beans, shelled

Fish stock (broth)

1 sprig of marjoram

Salt

Freshly ground white pepper

Pinchitos de Rape
Skewered Monkfish (Anglerfish)

These small seafood kebabs are very popular in Spanish seaside restaurants. On hot days, they are served with a glass of dry sherry or light white wine. *Pinchitos* may also be prepared with other kinds of firm-fleshed fish, such as swordfish or tuna. They taste even better cooked over hot coals on a barbecue.

300 g/10 oz monkfish (anglerfish)

1 red (bell) pepper

1 green (bell) pepper

2 garlic cloves

Juice of 1 small lemon, organically grown

1 teaspoon cumin

Freshly ground white pepper

Salt

3–4 tablespoons olive oil

8 short skewers

❶ Wash the monkfish (anglerfish), pat dry and cut into bite-sized cubes. Wash and deseed the peppers and cut into large pieces. Thread the fish and peppers alternately onto 8 short skewers.

❷ Peel the garlic clove and chop finely. For the marinade, blend the lemon juice with the garlic, cumin, pepper, salt and olive oil.

❸ Pour the marinade over the fish, cover and leave to marinate in a cool place or the refrigerator for at least 2 hours.

❹ Pat dry with kitchen paper (paper towels) and cook under a preheated grill (broiler) or in a frying pan. Turn the kebabs frequently to cook them evenly all over. Serve immediately.

Note: Cut the peppers slanting downwards away from the skin to prevent the cut edges from turning brown too quickly.

Serves 4, about 165 kcal per serving

Meat Tapas

You will have some difficult choices to make when preparing meat *tapas*, as all kinds of meat can be turned into these tasty appetizers. Depending on the occasion and how much time you have for preparation, you can choose from a range of delicious dishes, such as a cooked bean stew (see page 88), gypsy-style calf's liver (see page 99) or country chicken with olives and peppers (see page 94).

Mongetes con butifarra
White Beans with Butifarra

Catalans just love these small, spicy sausages. They are the northern counterpart of the much-beloved Andalusian fiery chorizo. However, throughout Spain, most restaurants offer both *butifarra* and chorizo as plain *tapas* – grilled (broiled) whole or sliced and fried. This is one of the best-known *tapas* recipes with *butifarra*.

4–8 fat sausages, depending on size (*Butifarra*)

Flour

1 garlic clove

Olive oil

250 g/8 oz (1 cup) canned haricot (white) beans

1 bay leaf

1 sprig of marjoram

½ bunch of flat-leaf parsley

Salt

Freshly ground white and black pepper

❶ If using small, fat sausages, cut into slices the thickness of a finger; larger ones should be cut in half or quartered. Dust evenly with flour.

❷ Peel and crush the garlic clove. Heat the olive oil in a pan and fry the sausage over a high heat until browned all over. Meanwhile, season the beans with the bay leaf, marjoram sprig and garlic.

❸ Mash 1 tablespoonful of the beans with a fork. Remove the pan from the heat, stir in the mashed beans and pour a little water or stock (broth) over them.

❹ Add the remaining beans to the pan and cook over a medium heat.

❺ Wash the parsley, finely chop the leaves and add to the beans. Season with salt and black and white pepper to taste just before serving.

Serves 4, about 590 kcal per serving

Morcilla frita
Fried Black Pudding

For this recipe, you could substitute German black pudding or even the genuine Spanish *morcilla* if you can source it. It is available in some delicatessens and specialist Spanish food stores. The best *morcilla* is made from the famous black pigs of Asturias in northern Spain.

250 g/8 oz black pudding

2 onions

2 tablespoons olive oil

1 teaspoon cumin seeds

1 small loaf of white bread

Salt

Freshly ground white pepper

❶ Remove the casing from the sausage and cut into thick pieces.

❷ Peel the onions and cut into rings. Heat the oil in a heavy-based pan and sauté the onion rings.

❸ Add the sausage slices and fry on both sides until cooked.

❹ Crush the cumin seeds. Season the sausage slices with the cumin, salt and freshly ground pepper.

❺ Cut the bread into slices and toast. Serve with the black pudding.

Serves 4, about 300 kcal per serving

Duelos y quebrantes
Scrambled Eggs with Chorizo and Jabugo

Literally translated, *Duelos y Quebrantes* – one of the legendary Don Quixote's favourite dishes – means 'pain and suffering'. This may be due to the red chorizo fats running into the egg white and yolk. This is a particularly delicious *tapas* dish.

❶ Slice the chorizo thinly, and cut the ham into cube. Fry the chorizo and ham in the olive oil in a heavy-based pan.

❷ Beat the eggs lightly with some salt and black and white pepper – the egg whites and yolks should not blend completely.

❸ Add the beaten eggs as soon as the chorizo and ham fats melt.

❹ Leave to cook until the eggs have thickened and set underneath, then remove from the heat, cover and stand for 5 minutes before serving.

Serves 4, about 140 kcal per serving

50 g/2 oz chorizo (spicy Spanish sausage)

30 g/1 oz Jabugo or Serrano ham

1 tablespoon olive oil

2 eggs

Salt

Freshly ground black and white pepper

Hígado de cordero a la Jerezana
Lamb's Liver in Sherry

If possible, serve the liver straight out of the pan, as it may become a little tough when reheated. Make sure that you buy only really fresh liver.

400 g/14 oz lamb's liver

2 teaspoons dry sherry

Olive oil

2 onions

75 g/3 oz (6 tablespoons) butter

Salt

Freshly ground white pepper

1 sprig of thyme

❶ Wash the liver, pat dry with kitchen paper (paper towels), then cut in half and slice very thinly. Place in a bowl and pour the sherry over it. Stir and leave to marinate in the refrigerator or a cool place.

❷ Cover the bottom of a frying pan with olive oil and heat.

❸ Peel and halve the onions, then slice and fry until golden brown.

❹ Drain the liver in a sieve and pat dry with kitchen paper (paper towels).

❺ Add the butter to the hot olive oil and quickly fry the liver – it should still be slightly pink. Remove from the pan and sprinkle with thyme leaves.

Serves 4, about 360 kcal per serving

Chuletas de cordero con aceitunas
Lamb Chops with Olives

Olives are one of the great natural ingredients of traditional Mediterranean cuisine. Pickled olives are still the perfect accompaniment to an aperitif, whereas plain olives are added to salads and paellas. In this recipe, they are served with lamb chops which are cooked in a piquant sauce.

4 lamb chops

Salt

Freshly ground pepper

3 tablespoons olive oil

2 tablespoons sherry

2 tablespoons wine vinegar

100 g/3¹/₂ oz (1 cup) black olives, stoned (pitted)

8 fresh mint leaves

❶ Wash the lamb chops, pat dry with kitchen paper (paper towels) and season with salt and pepper. Heat the olive oil in a pan and briskly fry the chops on both sides.

❷ Pour the sherry and wine vinegar over the chops. Slice the olives finely, add to the pan and leave to simmer over a low heat for 5 minutes.

❸ Finely chop half of the mint leaves and add to the cooking sauce. When the sauce has reduced and thickened, serve the lamb chops in a pool of sauce, garnished with the remaining mint leaves.

Serves 4, about 370 kcal per serving

Cochifrito
Lamb with Lemon

This recipe is well-known in La Mancha, Aragón, Murcia and many other regions. Shoulder of lamb is the best cut to use. If you serve it as a *tapas* dish, aim to produce only a small amount of sauce.

1 Wash the lamb, pat dry with kitchen paper (paper towels) and then cut into cubes.

2 Heat the olive oil in a heavy-based casserole dish. Peel 4 garlic cloves, sauté in the pan and add the lamb.

3 Peel and slice the remaining garlic cloves. Peel the onions and chop them finely. Add the garlic, paprika and chopped onions as soon as the meat cubes are browned on all sides. Part-cover the casserole and leave to simmer over a low heat for 30 minutes.

4 Pour the lemon juice into the pan and turn up the heat.

5 Season with salt and pepper. Chop the parsley and add to the pan. Simmer for 10 more minutes over a very low heat.

Serves 4, about 400 kcal per serving

500 g/1lb shoulder of lamb

Olive oil

8 garlic cloves

2 onions

1 teaspoon mild paprika

Juice of 1$\frac{1}{2}$ lemons, organically grown

Salt

Freshly ground pepper

$\frac{1}{2}$ bunch of flat-leaf parsley

Rabo de buey estofado
Braised Oxtail

The preparation of this Andalucian classic dish is extremely time-consuming and should be done the day before as oxtail tastes best when reheated. It is often made on market days and public holidays but some *tapas* bars serve it regularly.

2 large onions

2 carrots

Olive oil

8 garlic cloves

2 large tomatoes

2 bay leaves

2 sprigs of thyme

1 kg/2 lb oxtail, cut into 5 cm (2 inch) pieces

Flour for dusting

3 tablespoons brandy

$^1/_2$ bottle robust red wine (350 ml/12 fl oz)

Salt

Freshly ground white and black pepper

❶ Peel the onions and carrots and cut into slices. Fry over a medium heat in hot olive oil in a heavy-based casserole dish. Meanwhile, peel the garlic cloves and chop finely. Pour some boiling water over the tomatoes, then skin, deseed and dice.

❷ Add the garlic, bay leaves and thyme leaves to the onions and carrots. Fry briskly and then fold in the tomatoes. Cook for a few minutes, then remove the vegetables from the casserole and keep warm.

❸ Heat some fresh olive oil in the casserole. Dust the oxtail pieces with flour, add to the hot oil and fry rapidly. Pour in the brandy.

❹ Stir in the braised vegetables and herbs and heat through before adding the red wine.

❺ Leave to simmer over a low heat for at least 3 hours. Add more red wine, if necessary. Season with salt and pepper to taste and serve the oxtail in its sauce.

Serves 4, about 270 kcal per serving

Hígado a la Asturiana
Calf's Liver Asturian-Style

Asturias is the most important milk-producing region in Spain. Few of its traditional dishes do not contain milk, cream, butter, veal or cheese. This unusual but tasty dish of strips of calf's liver is very popular and is often served as a *tapas* dish.

❶ Wash the liver, pat dry with kitchen paper (paper towels) and cut into slices. Pour the milk over it and set aside for 15 minutes. Drain the liver and pat dry with kitchen paper (paper towels). Dust lightly with flour.

❷ Cover the bottom of a heavy-based pan with olive oil. Fry the liver in the hot oil for 2–3 minutes. Drain and keep warm in a low oven.

❸ Peel and finely chop the onions. Pour some boiling water over the tomatoes, then skin, deseed and roughly chop them. Sauté the onions in the oil, then stir in the tomatoes. Cook for 2–3 minutes.

❹ Add the lemon juice and season to taste with salt and freshly ground pepper. Stone (pit) and slice the olives. Add half of the olives and the cream to the pan. Heat through gently without boiling.

❺ Pour the sauce over the liver, garnish with the remaining olives and serve.

Serves 4, about 400 kcal per serving

500 g/1 lb calf's liver

250 ml/8 fl oz (1 cup) milk

Flour for dusting

Olive oil

2 onions

4 tomatoes

Juice of 1/2 lemon

Salt

Freshly ground white pepper

100 g/3 1/2 oz (1 cup) green olives

125 ml/4 fl oz (1/2 cup) double (heavy) cream

Croquetas de pollo
Chicken Croquettes

Of all *croquetas*, chicken croquettes are the most popular. In northern Spain, croquettes are usually made with cod; in Andalucia it is ham; and in the Balearic Islands and Catalonia they use monkfish (anglerfish). You can adapt this basic recipe in many ways, using a range of ingredients.

❶ Wash the chicken, pat dry with kitchen paper (paper towels) and fry in a little olive oil for 8–10 minutes over a low heat. Remove and set aside.

❷ Melt the butter in the pan and add 1 tablespoon sifted flour. Stir with a wire whisk until the mixture thickens.

❸ Heat the milk and gradually add to the roux mixture, stirring constantly until you have a smooth, thick sauce. Season with salt, freshly ground pepper and nutmeg. Remove from the heat and set aside.

❹ Cut the chicken into very thin slices or mince in a blender and fold with 1 egg yolk into the white sauce.

❺ Beat the remaining egg yolk. Using a spoon, form 15–20 equal-sized portions out of the croquette mixture. Coat with flour, dip into the egg whites and beaten egg yolk and roll in the cornmeal. Fry the croquettes in hot olive oil until golden brown. Wash the oregano, finely chop the leaves and sprinkle over the croquettes before serving.

Serves 4, about 410 kcal per serving

For 15–20 croquettes:

300 g/10 oz chicken breasts, skinned and boned

Olive oil

15 g/¹/₂ oz (1 tablespoon) butter

2 tablespoons flour

250 ml/8 fl oz (1 cup) milk

Salt

Freshly ground white pepper

A pinch of grated nutmeg

2 eggs, separated

Cornmeal

¹/₂ bunch of oregano

1 onion

2 garlic cloves

3 tablespoons olive oil

150 g/5 oz spicy Spanish sausage (chorizo)

100 g/3¹/₂ oz Serrano ham

250 g/8 oz (2 cups) frozen broad (fava) beans

250 g/8 oz (2 cups) frozen peas

250 g/8 oz potatoes

1 sprig of thyme

250 ml/8 fl oz (1 cup) beef stock (broth)

Salt

Freshly ground pepper

Ground cinnamon

Ground cloves

Potaje de habas con chorizo
Bean Stew with Chorizo

This dish comes from Salamanca, yet it is also popular in Mallorca in a slightly modified version. Broad (fava) beans are braised with spicy Spanish sausage (chorizo), Serrano ham and vegetables to make a warming stew. For a really distinctive, spicy flavour, add a good pinch of ground cinnamon and some ground cloves just before serving.

❶ Peel and finely chop the onions. Peel the garlic cloves and cut into quarters. Heat the olive oil in a large pan and sauté the onion and garlic until golden. Thinly slice the sausage and dice the Serrano ham. Add to the pan and fry for 2 minutes.

❷ Stir in the broad beans and peas. Peel and slice the potatoes and add to the pan with the thyme. Stir in the stock (broth), then bring to the boil, cover the pan and simmer gently for about 30 minutes.

❸ Uncover and continue cooking for another 15 minutes or until a little of the liquid has evaporated.

❹ Remove the thyme and season the stew with salt and freshly ground pepper to taste. Add a pinch of ground cinnamon and a pinch of ground cloves, if wished. Serve hot with crusty wholemeal (wholewheat) bread.

Serves 4, about 380–570 kcal per serving

Conejo con salmorejo
Marinated Rabbit

In Andalucia, the home of this recipe, the fresh rabbit is cut into pieces and added immediately to the marinade.

❶ Cut the rabbit into serving portions, then wash and pat dry.

❷ Crush 4 peeled garlic cloves with the bay leaves, stripped thyme leaves and a pinch of salt in a mortar, or use a blender. Stir in the olive oil, mix well and pour over the rabbit. Turn several times in the marinade and leave in a cool place for at least 2 hours.

❸ Heat the marinade in a heavy-based casserole dish and add the rabbit pieces. Cook on all sides until golden brown. Add the rabbit's liver and cook for a few more minutes.

❹ Wash the pepper, deseed and cut into dice. Coarsely crush the remaining garlic cloves in a mortar or blender together with the peppers, paprika, cayenne, cumin and the liver. Blend with 1¹/2 tablespoons sherry vinegar and add some water or stock (broth).

❺ Add to the rabbit in the pan and leave to simmer over a low to medium heat for 40 minutes.

❻ Remove from the heat and stand for 15 minutes to allow the flavours to develop, then bring back to the boil, season to taste with salt and pepper and serve. It is also good served as a cold dish the following day.

Serves 4, about 320 kcal per serving

1 rabbit with its liver

8 garlic cloves

2 bay leaves

2 sprigs of thyme

Salt

Olive oil

1 red (bell) pepper

1 teaspoon sweet paprika

1 teaspoon cayenne

¹/2 teaspoon cumin seeds

Sherry vinegar

White pepper

Pollo al ajillo
Chicken with Garlic

This recipe is an Andalucian *tapas* classic. Instead of chicken, rabbit is often substituted. It is easy to prepare and does not take long.

500 g/ 1 lb chicken breast, skinned and boned

Flour for dusting

Olive oil

8 garlic cloves

2 teaspoons dry sherry

Salt

Freshly ground white pepper

1 lemon, organically grown

❶ Cut the chicken into bite-sized pieces. Wash and pat dry with kitchen paper (paper towels), then dust with flour. Peel and slice the garlic cloves.

❷ Cover the bottom of a heavy-based pan with olive oil. Heat the oil and fry the chicken and garlic until golden brown all over, stirring constantly.

❸ Pour in the sherry and simmer over a low heat for 10 minutes.

❹ Remove the pan from the heat, cover and stand for 15 minutes.

❺ Reheat briefly and season to taste with salt and pepper. Quarter the lemon and use to garnish the chicken.

Serves 4, about 320 kcal per serving

Albóndigas
Meatballs

These delicious meatballs taste best when they are served in a piquant tomato sauce.

❶ Put the bread roll in some warm water and leave to soak. Drain well.

❷ Peel the onion and garlic cloves, chop finely and sauté briefly in a pan with a little olive oil. Add the sherry and set aside.

❸ In a bowl, mix together the minced (ground) meat, eggs and drained bread roll. Add the onion and garlic mixture. Wash and finely chop the parsley and stir into the meat mixture. Season with salt and pepper.

❹ Form the mixture into balls, the size of a walnut, and dust with flour.

❺ Peel and crush the remaining garlic cloves. Heat the olive oil and garlic cloves in a pan. Add the bay leaf and meatballs and fry until cooked through and evenly browned.

Serves 4, about 510 kcal per serving

1 stale bread roll

1 large onion

6 garlic cloves

Olive oil

3 tablespoons dry sherry

350 g/12 oz (1^1/$_2$ cups) minced (ground) beef

150 g/5 oz (^{5}/$_8$ cup) minced pork

2 eggs, beaten

^{1}/$_2$ bunch of flat-leaf parsley

Salt

Freshly ground pepper

Flour for dusting

1 bay leaf

Habas tiernas con jamón
Tender Broad (Fava) Beans with Ham

This dish simply tastes wonderful when made with very young broad (fava) beans and smoked Jabugo ham, or with any other raw dried ham. The bars and *tascas* in Catalonia serve it with cooked ham in tomato sauce. However, they use frozen broad beans. The following version is delicious.

❶ Put the beans in their pods in a pan. Cover with cold water and bring to a boil. Boil vigorously for 8–12 minutes or until tender.

❷ Drain the beans and leave to cool until they can be shelled easily by hand. Just press them out of the pods.

❸ Peel and finely chop the onion. Heat the olive oil in a pan and sauté the onion until golden.

❹ Cut the ham into strips and add with the beans to the onion in the pan. Reheat, stirring constantly.

❺ Chop the marjoram leaves finely and stir into the beans and ham. Season with freshly ground white and black pepper.

Serves 4, about 440 kcal per serving

1 kg/2 lb young broad (fava) beans in their pods

1 onion

3 tablespoons olive oil

150 g/5 oz Serrano ham

1 sprig of marjoram

Salt

Freshly ground white pepper

Lomo en adobo
Marinated Grilled Fillet of Pork

Many Spanish butchers sell pork fillet in a spiced, aromatic marinade but this recipe shows you how to do it yourself. Small pork chops are sometimes lightly spiced, marinated and briefly grilled as an alternative to fillet. When served with a bread roll, this snack is called *pepiro de lomo*.

2 garlic cloves

Salt

1 sprig of marjoram, or pinch of dried oregano

1 sprig of thyme

1 bay leaf

1 teaspoon mild paprika

1/2 teaspoon cayenne

Freshly ground pepper

Olive oil

350 g/12 oz fillet of pork (pork tenderloin)

Crusty white bread

❶ Crush the garlic cloves in a mortar with a teaspoon of salt. Add the marjoram and thyme leaves, bay leaf, paprika and cayenne.

❷ Mix in the mortar and then stir in some freshly ground pepper and a dash of olive oil.

❸ Brush the pork fillet all over with the marinade, then cover with clingfilm (plastic wrap) and marinate in the refrigerator overnight.

❹ The following day, cut the pork fillet into 1 cm (1/2 inch) cubes and cook under a preheated grill (broiler) or in a ridged grill pan over a high heat, turning frequently. The pan or grill (broiler) must be very hot to allow the aroma of the marinade to blend with the meat.

❺ Serve immediately with some crusty white bread.

Serves 4, about 300 kcal per serving

Vegetable Tapas

For vegetarians or indeed anyone who simply loves fresh, crisp vegetables the Spanish cuisine offers an infinite variety of delicious vegetable *tapas*. Whether it is an exquisite aubergine (eggplant) pie (see page 138), stuffed avocados Andalucian-style (see page 106) or a mixed vegetable platter from la Mancha (see page 148), the finished dish will make the heart of every gourmet beat faster!

Aguacate estilo Andaluz
Avocados Andalucian-Style

For this *tapas* dish, the fresh avocados are marinated in some warm, spiced olive oil. The recipe comes from Andalucia.

200 ml/7 fl oz (⁷/₈ cup) olive oil

2 onions

4 garlic cloves

1 teaspoon cumin

1 teaspoon coriander seeds

¹/₂ bunch of flat-leaf parsley

A pinch of hot cayenne

Sherry vinegar

Salt

Freshly ground white pepper

4 small avocados

❶ Heat the olive oil in a pan. Peel the onions and garlic cloves, chop finely and sauté until golden brown.

❷ Crush the cumin and coriander. Wash and finely chop the parsley. Add the coriander, cumin, paprika and parsley to the pan and stir in a dash of sherry vinegar. Season to taste with salt and pepper. Remove from the heat and set aside.

❸ Cut the avocados in half and remove the stones (pits). With a sharp knife, carve a star around the cavity in each half.

❹ Spoon the hot, spiced olive oil into the cavity in each avocado half. Leave to marinate for 20 minutes.

Serves 4, about 620 kcal per serving

Gratinado de berenjas
Aubergine (Eggplant) au Gratin

It's the Manchego cheese that gives this tapas dish its typical flavour. If you fail to get Manchego, you can use some hard Swiss Emmental instead.

4 aubergines (eggplants)

Flour

Olive oil

750 g/1¹/₂ lb ripe tomatoes

1 garlic clove

1 teaspoon sugar

Salt

Freshly ground white pepper

4 albahaca sprigs (Spanish basil with small leaves), or 2 sprigs of basil (with large leaves)

150 g/5 oz Manchego cheese (or use Emmental cheese)

❶ Wash the aubergines (eggplants) and cut into 1 cm (¹/₂ inch) thick slices. Coat with flour and sauté lightly on both sides in some hot olive oil. Keep warm in a low oven.

❷ Wash the tomatoes and cut into pieces. Peel the garlic cloves, cut into small pieces and add to the pan with the tomatoes. Cook gently until you have a reduced tomato sauce.

❸ Season the sauce with sugar, salt and pepper. Cut the basil leaves into strips and add to the sauce.

❹ Cover the bottom of a casserole dish with a layer of the tomato sauce. Top with a layer of aubergine (eggplant) and continue alternating the layers.

❺ Grate the cheese and sprinkle over the top. Bake in a preheated oven at 180°C (350°F), Gas Mark 4 for 20 minutes until crisp and golden.

Serves 4, about 300 kcal per serving

Alcachofas a la parilla
Grilled Young Artichokes

The first young artichokes are sold in Spanish markets from March onwards. In some regions, they grow along the borders of fields. They may be recognized by the purple colour of their leaves. These, together with the tiny green artichokes, are the type used in this recipe. Large artichokes must be precooked before grilling (broiling).

1 Remove the outer leaves and tough ends of the artichokes and cut off the stems. Cut in half.

2 Place the artichokes, tops downwards, on a rack in a grilling (broiling) pan and grill (broil) under a high heat for 7–9 minutes.

3 Turn the artichokes over and sprinkle the tops with olive oil. Grill (broil) for 5–7 minutes.

4 Season with salt and pepper and sprinkle with lemon juice. Serve the artichokes tops upwards so that the delicious olive oil inside each one is not spilt.

Serves 4, about 210 kcal per serving

12 small young artichokes
Olive oil
Salt
Freshly ground white pepper
Juice of ¹/₂ lemon

Escalivada
Grilled Aubergine (Eggplant) and Peppers

Some tourists are amazed at the wide assortment of food that the Catalonians prepare over their charcoal burners – mostly meat and vegetables. Here is a recipe that can be cooked easily with or without a charcoal burner. It will bring an enchanting Spanish touch to your table.

4 red (bell) peppers

2–3 aubergines (eggplants)

2 garlic cloves

5 tablespoons olive oil

Salt

Freshly ground white and black pepper

Juice of 1 lemon, organically grown

❶ Wash the peppers and aubergines (eggplants) and pat dry. Preheat the oven to 230°C (450°F), Gas Mark 8. Arrange the vegetables on a baking (cookie) sheet lined with aluminium foil and roast, turning occasionally, until the skins are slightly charred all over.

❷ Remove from the oven and allow to cool a little, then skin and deseed the peppers. Cut the warm peppers and aubergines (eggplants) into strips and arrange on a serving dish.

❸ Peel and crush the garlic cloves and mix with the olive oil, salt, pepper and lemon juice. Sprinkle over the roasted vegetables.

❹ Leave to marinate in a cool place for at least 2 hours.

Serves 4, about 210 kcal per serving

Patatas a la Riojana
Potatoes Rioja-Style

In Spain, potatoes are usually cooked together with other vegetables or they are added to a roast. They are seldom served as a side dish. This recipe from the renowned Rioja valley is also served as a *tapas* dish.

❶ Peel and quarter the potatoes or cut into 8 thin slices, depending on their size.

❷ Cut the chorizo into small pieces. Peel the onion and garlic cloves. Chop the onions and cut the garlic into thin slivers.

❸ Cover the bottom of a heavy pan with olive oil and heat. Fry the chorizo, onion and garlic over a high heat.

❹ Add a little more olive oil to the pan, then add the potatoes. Cook, stirring frequently, for a few minutes, then pour in a little stock (broth) and simmer over a low heat for 25 minutes.

❺ Season with salt and pepper, and serve.

Serves 4, about 360 kcal per serving

200 g/7 oz chorizo (spicy Spanish sausage)
500 g/1 lb potatoes
1 onion
3 garlic cloves
olive oil
vegetable stock (broth)
Salt
Freshly ground pepper

Pez de tierra
Aubergine (Eggplant) Purée

The literal translation of this dish is 'earthen fish'. This rather strange name dates back to mediaeval times when the periods of fasting lasted for more than six months in a year.

❶ Wash and dice the aubergines (eggplants). Peel and slice the garlic.

❷ Cover the bottom of a cast-iron pan with olive oil and heat. Add the aubergines (eggplants) and garlic, and sauté, stirring frequently, until the aubergines (eggplants) are tender.

❸ Purée the contents of the pan in a blender, or mash.

❹ Stir in a little olive oil, salt, freshly ground white pepper and cumin. Wash and chop the oregano and sprinkle over the purée. Serve with fresh white bread.

Serves 4, about 150 kcal per serving

2 aubergines (eggplants)
5 garlic cloves
Olive oil
Salt
Freshly ground white pepper
1 teaspoon ground cumin
2 sprigs of oregano

Tomates empanados fritos
Fried and Breaded Tomatoes

This dish was long known in Spain, even before it became famous in an American film. In the United States, green tomatoes are used; they should be ripe for this recipe.

❶ Wash the tomatoes and cut into thick slices. Season with salt and set aside to drain for about 30 minutes.

❷ Pat dry the tomato slices with kitchen paper (paper towels) and coat in the cornmeal.

❸ Wash and chop the marjoram. Beat the egg with the chopped marjoram and then dip the coated tomato slices into the egg and then back into the cornmeal.

❹ Press lightly with your fingers and then fry the tomatoes in some hot olive oil. Season with salt and serve.

Serves 4, about 450 kcal per serving

4 large beefsteak tomatoes
Salt
200 g/7 oz (1 cup) cornmeal
2 sprigs of marjoram
1 egg
Olive oil

Coliflor al estilo de Badajoz
Fried Cauliflower Badajoz-Style

Spanish cuisine has a lot of recipes with cauliflower. The following comes from the province of Estremadura.

3 garlic cloves
Salt
Freshly ground pepper
4 teaspoons sherry vinegar
1 small cauliflower
3 sprigs of flat-leaf parsley
3 eggs
Olive oil
1 bay leaf
Flour for coating

❶ Peel 2 garlic cloves and crush in a mortar with 1 teaspoon salt. Then stir in the pepper and sherry vinegar.

❷ Break the cauliflower into florets. Cut crossways into the thick stems from below and blanch the florets in boiling water for 4 minutes. Drain and add to the marinade.

❸ Leave the florets in the marinade for 30–45 minutes, stirring several times.

❹ Wash and finely chop the parsley. Beat the eggs, add the chopped parsley and season with salt and pepper.

❺ Heat the olive oil (3 fingers high) in a cast-iron pan. Take the remaining garlic clove between your thumb and forefinger and press open. Add to the pan with the bay leaf.

❻ Drain the florets, coat with flour and then with beaten egg, and fry in hot olive oil until crisp and golden brown.

Serves 4, about 270 kcal per serving

Tortilla de espinacas con berenjas
Spinach and Aubergine (Eggplant) Omelette

You need a very hot pan for this tortilla so that it is really golden brown on the outside, stays soft inside and releases its aroma. It only tastes half as good if it is overcooked.

1 Wash the spinach thoroughly, remove the stems and shred the leaves. Blanch in some boiling water, drain thoroughly in a sieve and keep warm.

2 Peel the aubergines (eggplants), quarter and slice. Fry in a little hot butter and olive oil in a cast-iron pan.

3 Stir in the drained spinach when the aubergines (eggplants) are just tender. Stir well and season with salt and pepper.

4 Beat the eggs and fold in the spinach mixture. Check the seasoning.

5 Heat a little olive oil in a heavy pan and cook the tortilla on both sides until golden brown. Use a plate to turn the tortilla over.

Serves 4, about 380 kcal per serving

100 g/3^1/$_2$ oz spinach
4 small aubergines (eggplants)
30 g/1 oz (2 tablespoons) butter
2 tablespoons olive oil
Salt
Freshly ground white pepper
8 eggs

Tortilla de verduras
Vegetable Omelette

This is another typical *tapas* dish which makes a pleasant change from the ubiquitous *tortilla Espanola*.

Olive oil

4 large potatoes

2 carrots

2 garlic cloves

2 small onions

4 artichokes

1/2 cauliflower, broken into florets

4 sprigs of flat-leaf parsley

3 sprigs of marjoram

8 eggs

Salt

Freshly ground white pepper

❶ Heat the olive oil in a cast-iron pan.

❷ Peel the potatoes, carrots and garlic cloves. Cut the carrots in half and slice with the potatoes and garlic cloves. Peel the onions and cut into rings. Break off the stems of the artichokes. Remove the tough outer leaves and use scissors to cut off the bristly ends of the leaves.

❸ Cut the artichokes into 8 thin slices. Add all the vegetables to the pan, and cook for a few minutes, then stir in the cauliflower florets. Cook for 3–4 minutes and remove from the pan.

❹ Drain on kitchen paper (paper towels) and set aside. Wash the parsley and marjoram and crush the leaves in a mortar.

❺ Beat the eggs and mix in the herbs and drained vegetables. Season with salt and pepper and pour into the hot pan.

❻ Fry the tortilla on both sides until brown, using a plate to turn it. The omelette should be soft inside and cooked and golden outside.

Serves 4, about 420 kcal per serving

Pimientos con nata
Creamed Peppers

In the province of Aragon, a particularly long, hot kind of pepper is made into an extraordinary dish which is famous throughout Spain. In this version, ripe red (bell) peppers have been substituted but you could add deseeded, chopped hot chillies for a more fiery result.

❶ Wash the peppers, pat dry with kitchen paper (paper towels) and roast in the oven at 230°C (450°F), Gas Mark 8 for 15–20 minutes, turning constantly so that the skin bursts and chars all over. Transfer to a china bowl, cover with a plate or lid and set aside for 5–10 minutes.

❷ Skin the whole peppers over the bowl to collect all the juices. Cut off the tops, scoop out the seeds and ribs, and cut the flesh into 5 cm (2 inch) wide strips lengthways. Keep warm in a low oven. Reserve the juices and press the ribs and tops in a sieve.

❸ Warm the cream – do not boil – and season with hot chilli powder, salt and a sprinkling of sugar (if using fiery hot pimentos, omit the sugar). Fold into the reserved pepper juices.

❹ Pour onto a preheated serving plate and arrange the warm pepper strips on top.

Serves 4, about 240 kcal per serving

4 red (bell) peppers

200 ml/7 fl oz (⅞ cup) crème fraîche or sour cream

Salt

Sugar

Acelgas con champiñones
Beetroot (Beets) with Mushrooms

In many *bodegas* and *tascas*, the *tapas* counters offer a wide selection of vegetables. The daily choice is determined by what is on offer in the local market that morning. Thus there is always a good range of seasonal vegetables. And some of these become classic *tapas dishes*.

750 g/1¹/₂ lb yellow beetroot (beets)

250 g/8 oz mushrooms

2 onions

2 teaspoons dry sherry

3–4 tablespoons olive oil

Salt

Freshly ground white pepper

❶ Wash the beetroot (beets) and remove the tops and leaves.

❷ Cook in a little water until the beets are tender, then drain well, cool and peel away the outer skin.

❸ Clean and slice the mushrooms. Peel and dice the onions. Heat the olive oil in a cast-iron pan and briskly fry the onions and mushrooms.

❹ Stir in the sherry. Cut the beetroot (beets) into strips and add to the pan.

❺ Toss all the ingredients well. Season with salt and pepper and serve.

Serves 4, about 140 kcal per serving

Troncos de acelgas rebozados
Breaded Beetroot (Beet) Sticks

Spain boasts of a large variety of breaded, shallow-fried and deep-fried vegetable dishes. This recipe features yellow beets.

cooked yellow beetroot (beets), peeled and cut into 12–16 sticks

Flour for coating

2 eggs

200 g/7 oz (1 cup) cornmeal

Olive oil

Salt

❶ Dry the yellow beetroot (beet) sticks on kitchen paper (paper towels).

❷ Coat lightly in flour, then in beaten egg and, finally, in cornmeal.

❸ Heat some olive oil (2 fingers high) in a cast-iron pan and fry the beet sticks until crisp and golden brown. Season with salt and serve.

Serves 4, about 440 kcal per serving

Champiñones rellenos
Stuffed Mushrooms

You may have a hard time picking your favourite mushroom recipe in Spain where mushrooms are stuffed with almost anything you can think of. In southern Spain, mushrooms are sometimes stuffed with chorizo, the spicy red sausage, whereas in other areas a minced (ground) meat filling prevails. In this recipe, we have used minced (ground) beef but you could use pork or even lamb instead.

❶ Soak the bread roll in some warm water, then squeeze out the moisture. Peel the onion and both garlic cloves and chop finely. Fry quickly in some hot olive oil in a pan, add the sherry and set aside.

❷ Pour some boiling water over the tomatoes, then skin and quarter. Discard the juice and seeds. Dice the remaining flesh and add to the pan.

❸ Wash and finely chop the parsley and add to the pan. Blend the minced (ground) beef with the eggs and soaked bread roll and fry in olive oil.

❹ Clean the mushroom heads and stuff with this mixture. Oil a baking (cookie) sheet and arrange the stuffed mushrooms on it. Cook in a preheated oven at 160°C (325°F), Gas Mark 3 for 10 minutes.

❺ Turn off the oven and leave the stuffed mushrooms inside for at least 10 minutes before serving.

Serves 4, about 280 kcal per serving

1 stale bread roll

1 onion

2 garlic cloves

2–3 tablespoons olive oil

4 teaspoons dry sherry

1 large tomato

2–3 sprigs of flat-leaf parsley

350 g/12 oz (1$\frac{1}{2}$ cups) minced (ground) beef

2 eggs

20–24 mushroom heads (depending on size)

Freshly ground pepper

Patatas al limón
Potatoes with Lemon

This combination of potatoes and lemons may seem a little strange at first but try this recipe – it's an extraordinarily refreshing dish for hot summer days in Andalucia or elsewhere.

500 g/1 lb small potatoes

Caraway seeds

Juice of 2 lemons, organically grown

200 ml/7 fl oz ($^7/_8$ cup) beef stock (broth)

200 ml/7 fl oz ($^7/_8$ cup) sherry vinegar

6 garlic cloves

1 bunch of flat-leaf parsley

Salt

Freshly ground white pepper

Olive oil

❶ Wash the potatoes and boil in their skins with a small handful of caraway seeds for 20 minutes. Drain well.

❷ Mix the lemon juice, beef stock (broth) and sherry vinegar in a bowl. Peel and finely chop the garlic cloves. Wash and chop the parsley. Season with salt and freshly ground pepper and stir into the marinade.

❸ Skin the hot potatoes and cut into 1 cm ($^1/_2$ inch) slices. Stir, while still warm, into the marinade and mix well. Leave to marinate.

❹ Add some olive oil, check the seasoning and serve. A chilled sherry *fino* makes an excellent accompaniment to this dish.

Serves 4, about 150 kcal per serving

Patatas bravas
'Brave' Potatoes

Here is another potato *tapas* – spicy fried potatoes Spanish-style. They are easy to make and have an exquisite taste.

500 g/1 lb potatoes
8 garlic cloves
3 hot fresh chillies
Olive oil
Salt
Freshly ground pepper

❶ Skin the potatoes and quarter or cut into 8 thin slices, depending on size. Pat dry with kitchen paper (paper towels).

❷ Take 4 garlic cloves and press open – do not peel. Cut 1 chilli into strips. Heat 250 ml/8 fl oz (1 cup) olive oil in a cast-iron baking pan. Wait until the oil almost starts smoking and then briskly fry the potatoes, garlic and chilli strips, stirring constantly until the potatoes are golden brown all over.

❸ Peel and thinly slice the remaining garlic cloves. Cut the remaining chillies into broad strips. Remove the hot seeds, if wished.

❹ Remove the garlic cloves and chilli pieces from between the fried potatoes, add a little more olive oil together with the sliced garlic and broad chilli strips,. Season with salt and freshly ground pepper and bake in a preheated oven at 180°C (350°F), Gas Mark 4 for about 35 minutes.

Serves 4, about 670 kcal per serving

Pisto Manchego
Mixed Vegetables from La Mancha

Pisto Manchego tastes best when spread chilled on to freshly toasted bread. After cooking, this vegetable dish resembles a thick paste. It is related to the French *ratatouille* and may be eaten warm or cold. This recipe calls for a few unpeeled garlic cloves. If you prefer to eat the *pisto* cold the following day, we recommend that you peel a few garlic cloves, crush them in a mortar and add them with a swig of olive oil to the dish. *Pisto Manchego* is also served with fennel seeds.

Olive oil

150 g/5 oz bacon

12 garlic cloves

3 tomatoes

1 red and 1 green (bell) pepper

1 courgette (zucchini)

1 aubergine (eggplant)

2 onions

Salt

Freshly ground white and black pepper

❶ Cover the bottom of a cast-iron pan with olive oil and heat. Dice the bacon and place with unpeeled garlic in the pan. Sauté until the bacon fat has melted, stirring constantly.

❷ Wash the tomatoes, remove the stems and cut into 8 thin segments. Wash the peppers and cut each into 8 slices. Wash the courgette (zucchini) and aubergine (eggplant), remove the stems and dice. Peel the onions and cut into strips. Stir the onions into the pan, followed by the remaining vegetables, finishing with the tomatoes. Sauté until cooked.

❸ When all the vegetables are well cooked, leave to simmer over a low heat for 30–40 minutes, stirring occasionally. Season with salt and freshly ground white and black pepper. A chilled strong white wine always goes well with this dish or, of course, a chilled dry sherry.

Serves 4, about 380 kcal per serving

Index

almonds, salted 37
aubergines (eggplants) 112, 114, 127, 138, 139
avocados 106

basic *tapas* 37, 87
béchamel sauce 83
beetroot (beets) 140
bread spread 149
bread tapas
- bread with oil and tomato 27
- bread with pork cracklings 20
- toasted white bread cubes 32
- tomato bread with ham 22
Butifarra 27, 72

cake tapas
- red pepper traybakes 136
calf's liver 85
Canadillas 39
carrots 150
cauliflower 120, 132, 133
cheese tapas
- cheese cubes, fried 29
- cheese from Mahón 41
- cream cheese balls 29
chicken 76, 87, 90, 94
chickpeas 114, 115
Chorizo 27, 72, 79, 88 117, 143
cod 50, 58
courgettes (zucchini) 31
cream cheese balls 29

dates with bacon 39
'Don Quixote's favourite dish' 79

'Earthen Fish' aubergine (eggplant) purée 119
egg tapas
- eggs Sóller style 41
- eggs with peppers 38
- omelette with lamb's kidneys 74
- scrambled egg with Chorizo and Jabugo 79
- prawn (shrimp) and artichoke omelette 56

- vegetable omelette 130
Embutidos 27
Ensaladilla-pyramid 129
Fabada 27
fish tapas
- anchovies, fried 21
- cod balls 48
- cod croquettes 50
- fish, fried 51
- gambas, fried 26
- gambas with garlic 24
- hake with cider 58
- monkfish (anglerfish) Galicia-style 52
- monkfish (anglerfish), skewered 68
- mussels marinated in parsley and pine nuts 66
- octopus Galicia-style with paprika 53
- sardines, coated Santander-style 63
- sardines, fried 27
- sardines, marinated 34
- sardines with capers 57
- sardines with tomatoes 55
- scallops in garlic sauce 38
- scallops in sherry 35
- shark, yellow 60
- prawn (shrimp) and artichoke omelette 56
- squid with fresh broad (fava) beans 65
- tuna spreads 62
- tuna with courgettes (zucchini) and peppers 67

goat (young) 101
ground (minced) meat 143

hake 50, 58

Jabugo 79, 97

lamb 80, 90
lamb's kidneys 100
lamb's liver 80

Manchego 29
meat tapas
- chicken breast in sherry and almond sauce 76
- chicken croquettes 87

- chicken with garlic 90
- chicken with olives and peppers 94
- fillet of pork, grilled, marinated 102
- goat (young) with chickpeas 101
- lamb chops with olives 82
- lamb with lemon 83
- meatballs 93
- meat kebabs, Moorish 95
- oxtail, braised 84
- rabbit, marinated 89
Migas 32
monkfish (anglerfish) 52, 58, 68
Morcilla (black pudding) 78
mushrooms 108, 140, 143
mussels 61, 66

octopus 53
olives, spiced, pickled 27
omelettes 74, 151, 127, 147
oxtail 84

peppers (bell) 135, 136
- and courgettes (zucchini) with aioli 31
- grilled 116
- marinated 30
- pepper omelette 40
peppers (bell), marinated 40
pilgrim scallops 37
pinchitos 95
pluck tapas
- calf's liver Asturian-style 85
- chicken/goose liver with sherry 75
- lamb's kidneys in sherry 100
- lamb's liver in sherry 80
- liver, marinated 98
- omelette with lamb's kidneys 74
- veal sweetbreads gypsy-style 99
pork 102
pork cracklings 20
pork cracklings with Gofio 20
potatoes 144, 145
potatoes, fried (Spanish-style) 145
prawns (shrimp) 24, 26

rabbit 89, 90
redfish 51
regional specialities
- Andalucia 39, 55, 65, 72, 84, 87, 89, 90, 94, 95, 106, 150, 139, 144

Spanish recipes

Concept and realization:
Meidenbauer • Martin Verlagsbüro,
Munich
Text and recipes: Anja Werth,
with recipes by Food Lock Studio
Editor: Nina Jane Merrens
Layout and typesetting: Hubert
Grafik Design, Munich
Photographs: Brigitte Sporrer,
Alena Hrbkova
Food styling: Hans Gerlach
Cover design: BOROS, Wuppertal
Printed and bound by Druckerei
Appl, Wemding

© 2000 DuMont Publishing
Cologne
(monte von DuMont)
All rights reserved

ISBN 3-7701-7003-2

Printed in Germany

The content of this book has been
thoroughly researched. Neither the
author nor the publishing company
can accept responsibility for the
information.

Acknowledgements: The editors
and publishing company are most
grateful to BodaNova, Sweden;
Culti, Munich; Impressionen
Versand, Wedel; Rosenthal Studio-
Haus, Munich
for their support while making this
book.
BodaNova, Sweden: 54, 94, 108,
134, 142
Culti, Munich: 73, 126
Rosenthal Studio-Haus, Munich:
142
Impressionen Versand, Wedel:
40,99

**A word about the
photographers:**
Brigitte Sporrer and Alena Hrbkova
met during their photographic
training in Munich. After assisting
several commercial and food
photographers, they now work in
their studios in Munich and Prague.

A word about the food stylist:
Hans Gerlach is a professional cook
and architect from Munich and
works as a freelance food stylist.
Most of his clients are in the print
and TV commercial business. He is
also the co-author of several
cookery books.